THE ALPS
AND THEIR PEOPLE

Susan Bullen

Wayland

PEOPLE
· AND PLACES ·

The Alps and their People

The Amazon Rainforest and its People

The Arctic and its People

The Ganges Delta and its People

Islands of the Pacific Rim and their People

The Mediterranean and its People

The Prairies and their People

The Sahara and its People

First published in 1994 by Wayland (Publishers) Ltd
61 Western Road, Hove, East Sussex, BN3 1JD, England

© Copyright 1994 Wayland (Publishers) Ltd

British Library Cataloguing in Publication Data
Bullen, Susan
 Alps and Their People—(People &
 Places Series)
 I. Title II. Series
 949.407

ISBN 0 7502 0873 2

Typeset by Dorchester Typesetting Group Ltd
Printed and bound in Italy by G. Canale & C.S.p.A.

Book editor: Alison Field
Series editor: Paul Mason
Designer: Mark Whitchurch

Consultant: Dr Tony Binns is a geography lecturer in the
School of African and Asian Studies at the University of
Sussex and geography tutor for the university's teacher
training course.

Cover: The village of Telfes, in the Austrian Tyrol. The peak
of Kalkkogel (2,808 m) is in the background.

Title page: Many Swiss towns are built around rivers and
lakes.

Contents page: Typical paintings decorate an old house in
the Bavarian Alps, in Germany.

Acknowledgements: The author would like to thank Neil Hadden
for his contribution to this book.

The publishers would like to thank the following for allowing
their photographs to be reproduced in this book:
Bruce Coleman Ltd 9 (Crichton), 11, 36 (main) (Henneghien),
40 (Davies), 42 (Cramm), 43 (Reinhard); C. M. Dixon 23;
Eye Ubiquitous 12 (Burrows), 15; Life File 24; John Cleare/Mountain
Camera 5, 8, 16 (both), 33 (both), 37 (O'Connor); Mary Evans
Picture Library 13, 29 (both); Swiss Tourist Office 28; Wayland
Picture Library title page, contents page, 22 (inset), 25 (inset), 26, 27
(both), 31, 36 (inset); ZEFA cover, 6 (Damm), 7 (Davidson), 11, 18,
19, 20 (Ebersberg), 21 (Buchner), 22 (main) (Hieberler), 25 (main)
(Rossenbach), 30 (Streichan), 32 (Boesch), 35, 38, 41 (Keystone), 44
(Havlicek), 45 (Leidmann).
Artwork by Peter Bull (4, 17) and Tony Smith (10, 14–15, 34, 39).

C O N T E N T S

· THE · DRAMA · OF · MOUNTAINS ·

At the heart of western Europe lies a formidable barrier of rock, ice and snow that runs from Mediterranean France through Switzerland and along the southern border of Germany to eastern Austria. Passing through seven different countries, this network of peaks, valleys, rivers and glaciers forms a dramatic crescent, some 1,200 km long. What is this vast geological feature? We call it the Alps, which simply means the mountains.

The Alps are the highest mountains in western Europe. Their tallest peak, Mont Blanc, rises to 4,807 m – that's about half the altitude of Everest, the world's highest mountain. The Alps pass through France, Switzerland, Italy, Germany, Austria, Slovenia and Liechtenstein – a tiny principality with 25,000 inhabitants (about the size of a small town). In France, Germany, Italy and Slovenia, the mountains take up just a small proportion of the land area. In Switzerland and Austria, the mountains have made their mark on the national culture, while tiny Liechtenstein is completely dominated by the mountains.

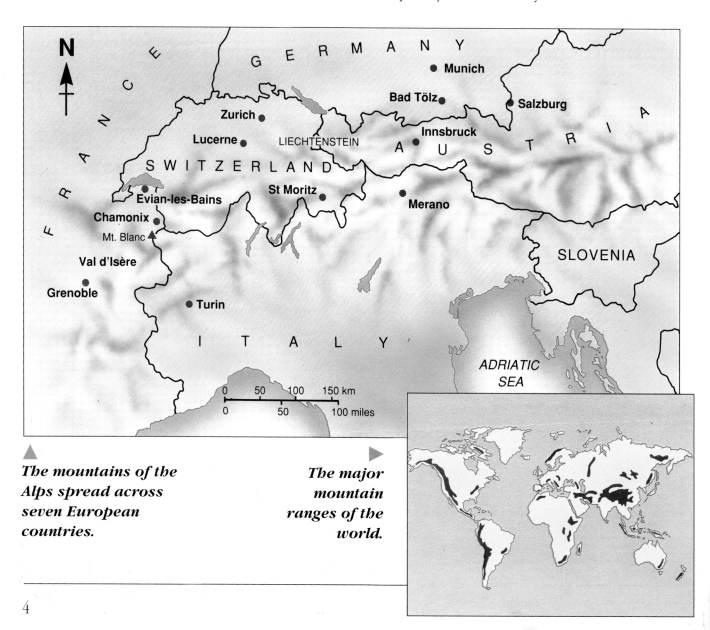

The mountains of the Alps spread across seven European countries.

The major mountain ranges of the world.

A stream flows over a rock face in the French Alps. In the background is the glacier known as the Mer de Glace (Sea of Ice).

THE BIRTH OF THE ALPS

Solid and eternal as they may appear, the Alps are not as old as the earth. In fact, compared with the estimated age of our planet, about 4,600 million years, the Alps are very young. They were formed only in recent geological time.

About 180 million years ago, the surface of the earth looked very different from today. All the continents were fused together in one supercontinent called Pangaea. Gradually, Pangaea broke up, first into two huge land masses, Gondwanaland and Laurasia. Then the continents broke up further and gradually, over millions of years, Africa made its way northwards towards the Eurasian land mass.

About 45 million years ago, Africa collided with Eurasia. The impact was enormous, crushing and squeezing bands of rock into dramatic folds. These folds of rock were pushed high above the earth's surface and so a new mountain range was formed – the Alps. The Himalayan range was created at about the same time, when the subcontinent of India collided with Asia.

Scientists think that the Alps are still growing today, although this process is offset by the constant erosion that wears rock down.

The geology of the Alpine region is extremely varied. Some of the mountains are formed from hard, igneous rocks from deep within the earth's crust. Some of these rocks have been metamorphosed under pressure to form slate and gneiss. Then there are sedimentary rocks, such as limestone. The most famous limestone mountains in the Alps are the dramatically weathered pinnacles of the Dolomites in northern Italy.

Water, in various forms, is abundant in the Alps. The mighty Rhine and Rhône rivers rise in central Switzerland, while the Po rises in the Italian Alps. Typical Alpine rivers are fast-flowing, their milky-green waters swollen each spring by huge volumes of melting ice and snow. Some mountain streams tumble off sheer rock faces, creating spectacular waterfalls. By contrast, the many lakes that are found throughout the Alpine area are still and tranquil, and are usually a beautiful, rich, deep green.

AN ICY LANDSCAPE

Dotted around the Alps are impressive glaciers – vast, slow-moving tongues of ice that occupy high valleys around the towering mountains. The most spectacular is the Swiss Aletsch Glacier, which stretches some 20 km and has an area of about 100 square km. In the French Alps, the largest glacier is the Mer de Glace ('Sea of Ice') near Mont Blanc.

The glaciers that remain in the Alps today give us some idea of what the landscape looked like during the last Ice age, over 18,000 years ago. Then all the valleys were filled with ice. The tremendous weight and pressure of the ice carved away the edges of the rock, creating rounded, U-shaped valleys. When the climate grew warmer and the ice began to melt, lakes formed as the excess water gathered in hollows gouged by the glaciers. The many lakes found in the Alps today remind us of its glaciated past, as do piles of rock debris called moraines, which were transported by the mighty glaciers.

WEATHER AND CLIMATE

Mountains are unpredictable places. Weather conditions often change quickly and dramatically. Low cloud can suddenly envelop a mountainside in a thick blanket of fog, while the gathering of clouds can signal an advancing thunderstorm. At high altitudes, snow or hail showers can never be ruled out. Avalanches, landslides and rockfalls are other hazards of the mountains. Avalanches are most frequent in spring, when snow starts to melt, suddenly releasing a huge volume of snow that rolls down the mountainside, gathering momentum and carrying rocks and trees down the slope. Avalanches can reach 300 kph and have caused extensive damage, as well as the deaths of many people. It is estimated that about 20,000 avalanches occur every year in the Alps.

The Alpine climate is marked by sharp contrasts. Winters are long and cold, lasting from November to late March or into April in the valleys. Heavy snow is the norm, and mountain roads can stay blocked for weeks or even months. The southerly fringe of the Alps, in the Italian South Tyrol and in the Italian part of Switzerland, Ticino, escapes the coldest winter weather. Here the climate

The Aletsch Glacier in Switzerland is gradually sliding down the mountain and wearing away the rocks beneath it.

An avalanche near the Swiss village of Grindelwald has swept over these trees.

A summer storm brewing in the granite mountains of the Swiss Alps.

is more Mediterranean in feel, allowing palms and subtropical vegetation to survive. Summers are warmest in these parts of the Alps, where the average temperature is 24 degrees Celsius (24°C). In fact the generally mild climate in the southern Alps enables people to grow vines on the sunny slopes, something that is impossible in the cooler northern parts of the Alps.

Prevailing westerly winds bring moist air masses from the Atlantic Ocean over the Alps. These condense into clouds when they meet the mountains, and fall as rain, especially on the exposed mountains of the western and northern fringes, in France and Bavaria (Germany). Other valleys, such as the Valais, in Switzerland, are shielded from much of the rain by the ridges of mountains to the west, and so are much drier.

The Alps are known for a characteristic warm, drying wind that blows from north to south. It is called the Föhn (pronounced 'fern') and can cause local whirlwinds in the Alps. Some people feel very uncomfortable when this wind blows.

A prolonged spell of warm weather in summer often leads to a mountain thunderstorm. Warm air masses cause the build-up of towering cumulonimbus clouds, which are trapped in the mountains. A dramatic thunderstorm in the Alps is exciting to watch (from a safe place) as flashes of lightning illuminate the outlines of the mountains and are then followed by torrential rainstorms.

·THE·LIVING·MOUNTAIN·

At first sight, a mountain appears to be a vast, uniform mass of rock and very little else. But in fact a mountain is a complex living system that changes a great deal from base to summit. For every 200 m of altitude, the temperature drops by about 1°C, and this has a marked effect on living things. We can divide a mountain into separate zones, each with its own character and wildlife.

THE LOWER SLOPES

This section of a mountain stretches from the valley floor to about 1,500 m above sea-level. The area is usually covered by deciduous forest, such as beech, oak and maple, interrupted only by wide streams that have wound their way down the mountainside. The trees provide homes for squirrels and birds, from song-birds to woodpeckers, owls and the crow-like nutcracker, a special bird of the Alps. Today, deer are the only large mammals likely to be found in these forests, although hundreds of years ago there were wolves and bears.

Gradually the deciduous trees give way to conifers, such as firs, pines, spruce and larch. A variety of shade-loving plants grow in these Alpine woods, including wood sorrel, wintergreens, hepaticas, Solomon's seal and wild raspberries and bilberries.

Sapphire-blue gentians are a typical plant of the high Alpine zone.

9

Mont Blanc 4,807 m

4,500 m

4,000 m

**Average max.
vegetation height**

3,500 m

**Small shrubs –
maximum height**

3,000 m

Minimum summer snow level

2,500 m   Average high pasture

Tree line

2,000 m

Average hay meadow level

1,500 m   Most deciduous trees – maximum height

1,000 m

500 m

Sea-level

THE LOWER PASTURES

Gradually, as we climb up an Alpine mountain, the forests thin out and change into open pastures, where cattle are grazed in summer. Many streams cut through the lush, lower pastures, creating boggy areas where water-loving plants thrive. These include marsh marigolds, primulas, marsh orchids, and the beautiful, starry white flowers of grass-of-Parnassus. The boggy pools are a perfect habitat for dragonflies and frogs.

THE UPPER PASTURES

At about 2,000 m, trees stop growing on the mountainside. This level is called the tree line, and beyond it is the realm of high pastures, where the soil is poor and the grass is kept short by strong winds. The only trees that survive at this level are gnarled dwarf pines or larches.

Where trees give up, the true Alpine plants take over. These small, resilient plants thrive on well-drained, sunny slopes at high altitudes. With their hairy or fleshy stems and leaves, they survive the biting winds and can withstand being buried under snow for much of the year. Many Alpine plants have rosettes of small leaves, which create a snug mound that keeps out cold winds and prevents moisture loss. There are deep-blue gentians, bright-yellow anemones, rose-pink alpine azaleas and brilliant orange-and-purple toadflax. In rocky outcrops, the famous grey-felted edelweiss flowers can be found.

These high pastures are the true Alpine zone of the mountain. Goats and sheep graze at this level, while native mammals called marmots stand guard at their burrows, whistling alarm calls if an eagle appears. These animals hibernate in their burrows during the long Alpine winter.

A marmot acts as lookout for other members of its colony. In winter, marmots hibernate in their burrows.

The vegetation on a typical mountain in the Alps changes as the altitude increases. On the highest mountains, the maximum vegetation height is higher than shown here.

The Matterhorn (4,478 m) is on the border between Switzerland and Italy. The snow at the top does not melt even in summer.

BEYOND THE SNOW LINE

The highest part of a mountain is a barren world of boulders, scree and sheer rock faces. This is the level of permanent snow, which in the Alps is between 2,500 m and 3,100 m. A few plants survive at this altitude, including the glacier crowfoot, reputedly the highest-growing of all Alpine plants. Several animals can be found in this Arctic-style wilderness, including birds such as alpine choughs, sparrow-like alpine accentors and snow finches. Occasionally, sure-footed chamois and ibex climb rocky outcrops at this level. Above them, golden eagles and buzzards circle in the sky.

·MOUNTAIN·SETTLEMENTS·

*I*t might surprise you to learn that people were living in the Alps as far back as 50,000 years ago. At that time there were Neanderthals living in caves in parts of Switzerland and Austria. They made fires to keep warm and hunted wild animals, but died out mysteriously some 30,000 years ago, perhaps as the climate grew colder. After the last Ice age came to an end about 10,000 years ago, modern humans flourished in the Alps. At first they lived in caves, where in places they left fascinating paintings on the rock. Later they lived in simple huts and grew their own food crops. They used axes to clear trees and scrub from the lower slopes and the valleys, creating fields where they grew grain, which they harvested with sickles. These people also kept goats, sheep, pigs and cattle, which made them the first Alpine farmers.

CHOOSING A SITE

If you found yourself in the Alps several thousand years ago, where would you choose to make a home? You would probably pick a valley, where the land is flat and easier to build on and to cultivate. The valley is a warmer place than the exposed mountainsides, and provides easy access to the lower slopes for firewood or to hunt animals. But which part of the valley would you choose?

A valley is broader at one end, called the mouth. The other end, the head of the valley, is much narrower, being enclosed by steep mountainsides. These block out much of the sun, making the head of the valley much shadier than the mouth. In winter, when the sun is low in the sky, the head of the valley can be a very cold, gloomy place. Some very

A nineteenth-century artist's idea of how early settlers in western Switzerland may have lived.

steep valleys are sunless in the depths of winter. Snow may lie in the head of the valley from early November until April. By contrast, the mouth of the valley enjoys much more sunshine on a winter's day. Snow does not lie on the ground for as long, and spring arrives several weeks earlier than in the head of the valley. The valley mouth provides easier access to neighbouring valleys, allowing better contact with other settlements.

Larger towns in the Alps are often at the mouth of the valley, or at the meeting of two valleys, for example Innsbruck (Austria), Bolzano (Italy), Grenoble (France), Chur (Switzerland) and Garmisch (Germany). Many settlements are on the south-facing side of a valley, because this is much sunnier than the north-facing side.

The Lauterbrunnen Valley

The Lauterbrunnen Valley is a large hanging valley nestling below Switzerland's most impressive mountains: the Eiger, Mönch and Jungfrau, which are all around 4,000 m high. There are settlements in various parts of the valley, all of which have their own characteristics.

Lauterbrunnen village lies in an open, sunny part of the valley. It is a good-sized settlement, with connections by railway to other valleys and by funicular railway to the high village of Wengen.

Stechelberg lies in the head of the valley. Here the valley is narrower and overshadowed by steep slopes. It is a long way from the mouth of the valley, and the settlement is much smaller

Jungfrau 4,158 m

Mürren 1,634

Stechelberg

Wengen 1,274 m

Grütschalp

Lauterbrunnen 796 m

than Lauterbrunnen. It has a few services, such as a school and a shop, plus a cable car up to the village of Mürren.

Wengen is situated above the Lauterbrunnen Valley at an altitude of 1,276 m. It lies on a gentle south-west facing slope, which is sunny and sheltered from strong winds. Its situation makes it suitable for cultivating hay meadows and keeping cattle. Wengen is connected to the valley by railway, and also has rail links up to the famous Jungfraujoch. Some 1,500 people live in this village, but there is room for 5,000 tourists.

Mürren is situated on the opposite side to Wengen. Its east-facing situation means it is less sunny than Wengen. Perched above steep cliffs, at 1,645 m, it is less suited to cultivation than Wengen. Mürren is connected by cable car both to the valley near Stechelberg and to the Schilthorn mountain above. About 450 people live in Mürren, although 1,500 tourists can stay there.

thorn 3,782 m

Schiltorn 2,971 m

A rack railway train climbs up from Wengen to the Jungfraujoch. The fences on the hillside in the distance help to prevent avalanches.

This little hamlet, called Zmutt, is perched above Zermatt in Switzerland at 1,935 m. It has no road for access by motor vehicles.

Living in mountains is never straightforward, whichever part you settle in. Mountains are physical barriers that impose themselves on people. A journey along Alpine roads, even in the late twentieth century, is never as simple as one along roads on flat land. The zigzag mountain roads feature hairpin bends and may be liable to rockfalls, flooding or ice patches. In winter such roads are often blocked by snow for several months, so that the remote villages that depend on mountain roads are themselves cut off. For example, the little village of Vallorcine in the French Alps is accessible by just one road. When the road is blocked in hard winters, Vallorcine is often cut off for about fifty days in winter.

LANGUAGES IN THE ALPS

Mountains also have a strong effect on the language people speak. People living on one side of a mountain barrier may speak a different dialect or even another language from people on the other side. In the Rhône Valley in Switzerland, for example, a mountain barrier divides French- and German-speaking parts of the country. Visitors to Austria and Bavaria encounter the strong regional accents of the German-speaking people. Swiss German is a very strong dialect that barely resembles standard German, since it has its own vowel sounds and grammar. And in different parts of the Swiss Alps, there are different dialects of Swiss German. So languages are very complex within the Alps.

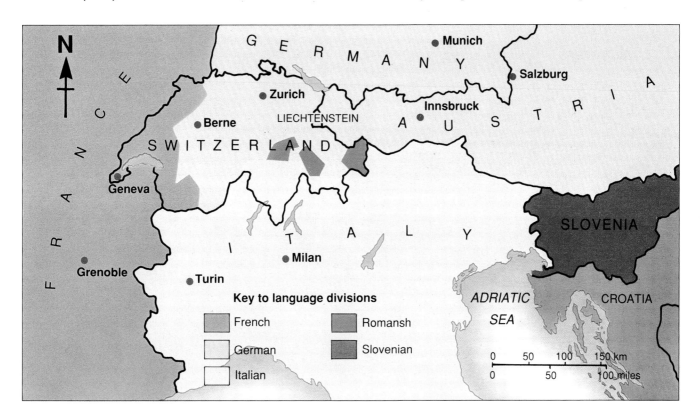

▲ *Most of the five languages spoken in the Alps have many different dialects.*

· USING · NATURAL · RESOURCES ·

*T*he Alpine region is by no means an easy place to live in. But the people who live there have always made the best of what their surroundings offer them. Natural resources – land, forests and water – can all be harnessed and used to advantage.

▲
Newly harvested hay is bundled up and dried in the sun near Mittenwald in Bavaria.

Crop-growing would be impossible in this rocky pasture, but cattle can graze here.

TAMING THE MOUNTAINSIDE

The valleys provide the most valuable land in the Alps. However, valleys make up just a small proportion of the land area – most of it consists of steep, unpromising slopes. A quarter of a typical mountain is occupied by rocks and scree, glaciers, snowfields, lakes and streams. And at least half of a mountainside is covered by forests and rough, high pastures, which lie under snow for much of the year. At best, just a quarter remains with suitable land for growing crops.

However, over the centuries, mountain dwellers have found a use for the seemingly barren grassland on the upper slopes. Although they cannot grow crops here, they can still produce food from these pastures – because poor pastures feed grazing animals and these feed people, with milk, cheese or meat. Sheep and goats happily graze the steepest upper pastures with poor soils and rough grass. Cattle are better suited to the lower, richer pastures, which are less steep. In the Alps, grazing animals are kept mostly for dairy products. Cheese-making was especially important in the past because it was a useful way to store milk, which would otherwise go off quickly. Cheese keeps much longer than milk. Today many Alpine farmers still make their own cheese.

While livestock graze the upper mountain pastures, the lower ones are kept as hay meadows. Here farmers grow a rich mixture of grasses and wild flowers, which are cut in early summer after they have set seed. The mown grass is dried in the sun and then the hay is stored in barns, ready to feed the animals during the long winter.

Meadows on the flat land in the valleys nearest the villages are reserved for growing crops such as maize, rye or vegetables, or for fruit trees.

These South Tyrolean farmers are enjoying a break from work.

THE ALPINE FARMING SYSTEM

The traditional method of farming in the Alps is a mixture of keeping grazing animals and growing crops. It is a very useful way of getting the most out of the various levels of the mountainside. But this traditional form of mixed farming is very labour-intensive. For three months in the summer, herders are needed to tend the flocks in the high pastures. However, summer is also a very busy time further down the mountain, where hay meadows are ready for cutting. To overcome the problem of managing crops and animals at the same time, traditional Alpine villages operate a communal farming system. About a dozen herders from the village are hired to look after everyone's animals. This leaves most other farming people free to deal with haymaking and tending the other crops, and

spares them the effort of going up into the very high grazing pastures.

Traditionally, high Alpine pastures are not owned privately but are shared among the villagers and their animals. It would be difficult to divide up these remote, rough pastures into small plots, and almost impossible to keep one family's animals out of another family's land. This is why communal herding works so well.

Today herding and haymaking are not as common as in the past. However, the dairy industry is still very important in the Alps, even though bigger dairy farms are replacing the much smaller traditional ones. Some hay meadows are still cut by hand, although the hay is often taken down the mountain by tractor, rather than by the old-fashioned horse and cart.

The Seasonal Migration of Livestock

Grazing animals such as cattle and goats cannot survive on the mountain all year round. So farmers time the arrival and departure of the animals to suit the seasonal changes in climate. Throughout the long winter, from late October to April, the animals are kept in barns in the valleys. They are fed on hay, which is harvested in summer from the hay meadows.

When spring arrives in late April, the animals are taken up the mountain in stages. First they spend several weeks in barns in the lush meadows of the lower slopes. As the snow melts higher up the mountain, the animals are moved to the lower pastures. Here they stay for up to a month. Finally, the sheep and goats are taken to the very high pastures to spend the summer there, from mid June to mid September.

Before the first snows arrive on the high pastures, from mid September onwards, the animals are moved down the mountain. They are taken down in the same stages, to reach the valley by the end of October. In many parts of the Alps, there is a procession as the animals return to the valleys. Bright flowers and ribbons are used to make decorative headdresses for the animals. This tradition shows the importance attached to grazing animals in Alpine villages.

▲
These cattle are being herded up an Austrian mountain.

Wood is an important Alpine building material, and it has been used to make these Swiss houses and fences.

These German foresters are felling timber.

FORESTS

For centuries, Alpine settlers have used the forested lower slopes to their advantage. Timber from the trees has been used extensively to build typical Alpine chalets and farmhouses. These homes always have a large, sloping snow roof made from tiles or slate. This keeps out snow and rain, which means that stored firewood remains dry when it is stacked close to the house. Before the advent of central heating, firewood was essential for keeping Alpine chalets warm. It was often burned in decorative tile stoves, which made a focal point for the home. Spruce, maple and beechwood from the forests were used for furniture such as tables, chairs, beds and large cabinets. In the past, almost everything for the home – from farming tools and milk pails to toys and ornaments – was made from wood.

Although there are other modern materials available today, wood is still widely used in Alpine homes. There are still Austrian and Swiss craftspeople who continue the traditional craft of woodcarving. Some produce carved wooden figures inspired by legends of the forest. In the Swiss Lötschen Valley (Bernese Oberland), villagers join processions at Candlemas, wearing grotesque or humorous face masks made by local woodcarvers.

MINERALS

Deep inside them, the Alps conceal another important resource – minerals. These are particularly abundant in the eastern Alps. Archaeological evidence shows that in 1800 BC, copper mines were being worked in the area of the Austrian Tyrol, and that a thousand years later, iron ore mines were worked in Austria and Slovenia. Austria was also the centre for salt and silver mining, both centred around Salzburg – the name means Salt Mountain. In the fifteenth and sixteenth centuries, Salzburg was a major mining area, employing many thousands of people. Even gold has been found in the Alps, especially in the Aosta Valley in Italy. Since the Industrial Revolution, coal and iron ore have proved more valuable.

Iron Age settlers in southern Bavaria used iron to make these knives.

· T R A D E · A N D · I N D U S T R Y ·

*T*raditional ways of making a living in the Alps, such as farming, are still important today, although the number of people who farm has fallen sharply since the 1950s. Mining has brought prosperity and growth to some parts of the Alps, although these benefits have declined as mineral deposits have been used up. So the region has had to find other ways to bring in much-needed income.

The textile industry has a long history, especially in Switzerland. In the seventeenth century, thousands of workers were involved, producing woollen and linen cloth. The industry flourished until the early twentieth century, when it declined because of changing tastes and competition from other countries. However, the small-scale industry that remains in Switzerland and Austria continues to produce the finest-quality cotton fabrics.

Quality is the key word for Alpine industry today. Over the centuries, Alpine people have realized that, because of their remote and difficult location, it is unwise to try to compete with other markets producing simple, everyday goods. Instead, they are more likely to be successful by selling quality specialist goods that are not widely produced everywhere else.

▶ *At Turin in Italy, factory workers manufacture Fiat cars.*

The grapes from these vineyards in the Italian South Tyrol will be used to make high-quality wine.

These factory workers are making business machines for Olivetti, in Ivrea.

So the Swiss are famous for making fine chocolate, unusual cheeses, precision instruments and of course quality watches from Geneva and the surrounding area. Swiss watches are reputed to be the finest in the world, in terms of quality and service. Alongside the luxury watches that cost many thousands of pounds, the Swiss also make colourful, modern watches designed for the young and less wealthy. Austria is known for its excellent optical goods and the crystal giftware from the Swarowski factory near Innsbruck.

The city of Turin, which lies just outside the Italian Alps, is an important industrial centre. It is the centre of the Italian car industry, and large Fiat and Lancia factories are based there. The car industry provides employment for many thousands of workers, some of whom live in the mountains. The town of Ivrea, a short distance from Turin at the edge of the mountains, is home to Olivetti, a company that makes business machines.

Good wines are produced in the sunnier areas of the Alps, such as the Rhône Valley in Switzerland and the South Tyrol in northern Italy. High-quality beer (lager) is brewed in many parts of the Alps, while distilled spirits are also widely produced. In the German-speaking countries they are called Schnaps.

Alpine Cheese

This Swiss cheesemaker is hoisting a curd-filled cheesecloth from a cauldron.

The dairy industry is still important throughout the Alpine region. Products made from Alpine cow's milk include butter and cream, but cheese is the most important dairy product. It has the advantage of keeping well and so can be easily transported over long distances, across the globe if necessary. In the past, people who owned a few cattle would make cheese to supply their own needs. People made cheese in various ways, sometimes using goat's or sheep's milk, and as a result there are a wide variety of cheeses from Alpine areas today.

Some cheeses, such as Swiss Emmental and Gruyère (cheeses with holes in) are exported all over the world. These cheeses are now produced in large factories, in which the curds (formed when the milk turns sour) are heated in huge cauldrons. The popularity of Swiss Emmental has prompted Austria and Bavaria (in Germany) to produce their own versions of the cheese. But Austria has a unique cheese of its

Many different varieties of cheese are sold at this stall in Munich, Germany.

The finished cheese is kept until it is mature and ready to sell.

own – Tiroler Graukäse, a cheese with a grey mould covering, produced in the Austrian Tyrol.

In the Savoy region of the French Alps, some cheeses are made from goat's milk. It is also here that the unusual cheese Tomme aux Raisins is made – a small, pressed cheese containing grape skins and pips. In the Aosta Valley region of Italy, the famous Fontina cheese is made. The most expensive and highly prized Fontina cheese is still made in the high Alpine pastures.

The importance of cheese to Alpine people is reflected in several traditional foods. The best-known is fondue, in which cheeses such as Gruyère or Fontina are melted with milk and sometimes the spirit Kirsch over a flame. Traditionally, several people share a pot of fondue, dipping pieces of bread into the rich mixture. The Swiss enjoy a simple dish called *raclette*, which is made by melting Raclette cheese over potatoes. In the French Alps, sliced potatoes are eaten with Gruyère cheese and onions, sometimes with cream added to them.

All of these simple dishes are rich and filling, and traditionally have been used as alternatives to meat.

The Swiss Textile Industry

Eastern Switzerland was once the centre of a thriving textile industry, based around the cantons of Glarus, St Gallen, Appenzell and Zurich. The Swiss trade in textiles began over 400 years ago and involved thousands of workers, mostly farming people who were seasonally employed. The industry started with cottage workers, who wove cloth or embroidered it in their own homes. In the nineteenth century, many large textile mills sprang up, especially in the Linn Valley, where they were powered by the waters of the River Linn.

The woollen, linen and cotton cloth was printed with characteristic, colourful designs that were influenced by the Orient. There was a great demand for these textiles until after the First World War, when fashions changed. From then onwards, most of the mills fell into disuse.

Today just a couple of mills print cloth in the Linn Valley. They produce a small number of traditional designs, plus modern printed fabrics for the fashion industry. The many empty mills in the valley stand like monuments to the region's productive past.

A traditional Alpine fabric.
▼

The greatest industry throughout the Alps today is based on selling a unique commodity – the Alpine scenery – to people from all over the world. The tourist industry has become very successful because people from outside the Alps are eager to experience the breathtaking beauty of the mountains at first hand.

ALPINE TOURISM BEGINS

Outsiders' enthusiasm for the Alps began in the middle of the nineteenth century, when people began to visit thermal springs at spa towns such as Evian les Bains in France, Bad Tölz in Germany, and Merano, a grand town in northern Italy. Then mountain climbing became popular and alpine clubs were formed in many European countries, with Britain the first in 1844. As climbing became more common, footpaths and rest huts were built on many mountains.

▲
The dangers of Alpine climbing are advertized in this 1906 poster.

▶
In 1870, visitors to Leukerbad in Switzerland enjoyed the thermal baths.

However, the Alps would probably have remained the preserve of the brave few, had it not been for some amazing feats of engineering. Towards the end of the nineteenth century, railways and tunnels opened up the mountains to people from outside. In 1882 the St Gotthard Pass was opened, after years of work by Italian, German and Swiss people. Now people could travel from northern Europe through the Alps. In 1898 a tramway was opened on Mont Blanc, as well as a cog railway leading from Zermatt past the Matterhorn and on to the Gornergrat, where tourists could see a new world of snow peaks and glaciers. And in 1912, people first had the chance to travel on a Swiss cog railway through the wall of the Eiger, to emerge at 3,454 m on the Jungfraujoch. This is still the highest railway station in Europe, and is one of the most spectacular and popular Alpine tourist highlights today.

In the 1930s people discovered that the Alps offered another thrill – skiing. At that time only the very wealthy could afford to ski, so it was not until the 1960s that mass ski-tourism began, when jet travel and package holidays became accessible to many more people.

The picturesque Kappellbrücke at Lucerne in Switzerland is an old fortified bridge.

This fairytale castle, Schloss Neuschwanstein, is a popular tourist attraction in Bavaria.

THE TOURIST BOOM

After the ski boom began in the 1960s, developers were keen to make the most of the 'white gold' – the snow that attracted the skiers. Soon resorts and ski lifts were appearing everywhere. The increase in tourists was staggering – for example, in 1970, the Austrian resort of Ischgl reported a fifty-fold increase in the number of overnight stays since the mid-1930s.

Today, as in the 1960s, there is a glamorous image to skiing. Some resorts, such as St Moritz in Switzerland, are still the preserve of the rich and famous. But there is certainly no shortage of resorts throughout the Alps. One of the biggest ski areas is Val d'Isère in the French Alps. But the biggest single event takes place in the Swiss Engadine. Every March a cross-country ski marathon takes place, with over 10,000 entrants.

Until the mid-1980s, the demand for skiing seemed insatiable. But then the numbers of skiers began to decline, notably in the French Alps. One reason must be that people were beginning to feel the effects of the economic recession. Another is that in the late 1980s Alpine resorts were hit by a shortage of snow during exceptionally mild winters. However, plenty of skiers still go to the Alps today, which makes the winter very much the high season.

Summer takes visitors to the Alps for different reasons. Many go to enjoy the spectacular scenery in warm weather and to see the sights, from small villages to elegant shopping towns. For many, a trip on a lake steamer or a literally breathtaking cable-car ride is not to be missed. Tourists in Bavaria flock to the fairy-tale baroque castles built in the 1870s for the eccentric King Ludwig II. Every ten years the German village of Oberammergau is the venue for a world-famous Passion play, centred on the last days of Jesus Christ.

▶

Many climbers enjoy the challenge of reaching the summit of the Eiger in Switzerland, at 3,970 m above sea-level. If such attractions become too crowded, people may decide to go elsewhere to climb.

◀

Rock climbing in the Alps is exciting but extremely challenging; this climb is for the experts only.

Walking and nature holidays are becoming more popular in the Alps. Many people enjoy staying in small mountain villages with no roads, served only by a funicular railway. Other summer visitors enjoy sports, ranging from rock climbing and mountaineering to hang-gliding and parascending from mountaintops over the valleys.

Tourism is certainly the cornerstone of the Alpine economy. It has brought prosperity and employment to mountain communities. For example, many construction workers have been employed to build hotels and holiday flats and to construct transport networks, such as cable-car routes, requiring massive steel girders to be set into the mountainside.

Local workers are needed to staff hotels, restaurants, shops, banks and tourist information centres.

However, tourism is not without its critics among the local people. Some people feel that it has spoiled the charm of remote villages. Certainly coachloads of tourists pour into traditionally quieter parts of the Alps, such as the beautiful Dolomites in northern Italy. Local people may also resent the fact that tourist facilities shut down in the low season. For example, cable cars usually run only during the peak of the winter and summer seasons. For the rest of the year, local people must manage without them. Sometimes tourism is blamed for spoiling the architectural character of a village. For example, the extensive ski centre around Val d'Isère in the French Alps has brought unattractive concrete developments. And visitors to the Zugspitze, Germany's highest mountain, may be shocked to find that the summit is dominated by large buildings – although these are there only because tourists want to enjoy restaurant facilities on a mountaintop.

Tourism is not a guaranteed source of income, either. It will survive only as long as people choose to go to the Alps, rather than to other places. Other mountainous parts of

A long queue for the ski lift at Tignes Val d'Isère.

the world are growing in popularity, such as the North American Rockies and the mountains of eastern Europe and New Zealand. And trekking in Nepal to see Mount Everest is now enjoyed by thousands of people.

Political events can affect tourism, too. The mountains of Slovenia, for example, used to be very popular with tourists. However, the outbreak of war in former Yugoslavia brought tourism to a halt.

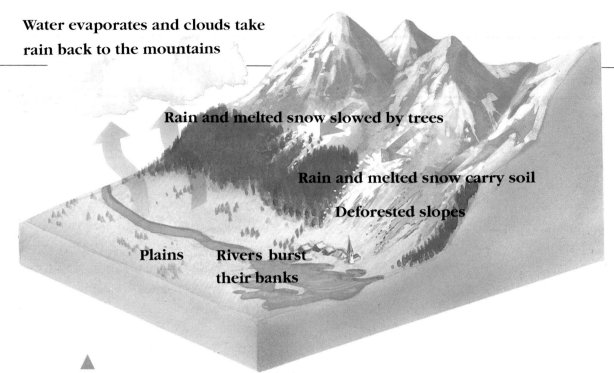

Water evaporates and clouds take rain back to the mountains

Rain and melted snow slowed by trees

Rain and melted snow carry soil

Deforested slopes

Plains   Rivers burst their banks

If trees are cut down for ski runs, the fragile slopes are left exposed.

THE PRICE OF THE PISTE

Since the early 1970s, ski resorts have sprung up all over the Alps. The Rhône-Alps area of France is the world's biggest skiing centre, and its biggest resort, La Plagne, alone boasts 119 ski runs and 112 ski lifts. Ski runs, or pistes, cover a huge area of the Alps – in fact, Austrian environmental groups have claimed that their country's ski runs stretch further than its railways! Such a wealth of ski areas is great news for winter sports fans, but bad news for the natural environment.

Most ski runs are on the middle slopes below the tree line. To create them, wide swathes of mountain forest must be cut down. The trees protect the slope against torrential rains and avalanches. Their root system anchors the soil and absorbs rainfall, while ground vegetation helps to hold back falling debris and floods. Without trees, a slope is left exposed and its topsoil is often washed away. Worse still, the slope is prone to the dangers of avalanches and mudslides.

The Alpine area has already suffered the consequences of removing the natural forest cover. On 20 July 1987, after torrential rain, floods and a mudslide swept down a mountain slope above the Italian village of Tartano. As a result, twenty people were killed, and roads, bridges and powerlines were wrecked. Many people think that the removal of forest to make way for ski runs caused this disaster.

Similar damage has occurred in Austria and Switzerland, prompting environmental groups to call for an end to the forest destruction. In some ski resorts, concrete barriers have been built to protect the village against avalanches. People have also tried installing drainage channels, to divert the flow of water as it pours down a bare slope. However, such measures are very expensive and do not entirely solve the problem.

It is now possible to ski all year round on dramatic Alpine glaciers. But here, too, the impact of skiers affects delicate soils and Alpine plants. It seems that as long as skiing remains popular, the natural environment must bear some of the cost.

·TWENTIETH·CENTURY·ALPINE LIFE·

*L*ate twentieth-century life has caught up with many parts of the Alps, although there are still small rural pockets that have changed little since the Second World War. Today the Alps are full of contrasts. There are thriving, modern economic centres such as the French city of Grenoble, with its new research industries and university. Then there are the historical, prosperous cities such as Geneva and Salzburg, which are popular financial and cultural centres. A stage down in size are the small towns such as Innsbruck, Garmisch and Chamonix, which are popular tourist centres. Finally, there are the small villages that have changed little because of their remote location.

In some cases, traditional communities exist side by side with their more modern counterparts. In the Aosta Valley, on the border of France and Italy, there are some remote valleys untouched by tourism. Here a small number of people continue to speak Valdostanisch, a dialect, while most people speak the official Italian language.

Languages play an interesting and central part in the Swiss national culture. There are three official languages – German, French and Italian – plus a fourth language, Romansch, spoken in Engadine in the south-east of the country. The three official languages appear on all official documents and on items sold in supermarkets. Younger Swiss people are often competent in several languages, although the older generations tend to speak just one. Thus language represents one aspect of change in the Alps.

▶

The town of Innsbruck in Austria. There are cities and towns of various sizes in the Alps. Some, such as Grenoble and Geneva, have their own industries. Others, such as Innsbruck, rely mostly on tourism.

This street in the Swiss town of Biel has German and French names.

Every winter, the Swiss town of Lucerne celebrates carnival time with musical street processions.

ALPINE TRADITIONS

Alpine customs used to form the core of community life but today, as in many parts of the world, they are fading fast. A number of traditions are associated with birth, marriage and death. Today it is still common practice to display photographs of a dead person outside the local church and on notices in the street. Traditional village weddings featured a procession from the bride's home to the church, and after the ceremony there was a splendid feast and dancing to folk music. Today this still happens, although pop music may replace the traditional music.

Ceremonies and processions linked to the religious calendar still take place – for example, on Palm Sunday, at Easter and Corpus Christi and on Ascension Day. There is also dancing around the maypole, and at New Year a procession of people in huge, illuminated headdresses, to ward off evil spirits during the coming year. The most popular celebrations take place at Fasching or Mardi Gras, before Lent begins. In the German-speaking countries especially, people dress up in elaborate costumes with masks and celebrate all night long.

Part of the Alpine culture is the wearing of a traditional costume. For men this consists of breeches, a waistcoat, jacket and hat. The women wear a wide, swinging dress (dirndl) with an apron, a white puff-sleeved blouse, an embroidered bodice and sometimes a bonnet or hat. Traditionally, each region of the Alps had its own distinctive costume, in particular colours and characteristic fabrics.

A woman in the Hèrens valley makes hay wearing traditional costume. She is probably part of the tourist industry: today it is unusual for people to wear traditional outfits except for special occasions or for tourism.

Today there are still young women who make their own costume, although they can now be bought in many village boutiques. Such designer outfits are available in a great variety of fabrics and colours, and people buy the one that appeals to them, rather than the one that represents their village or region.

Today Alpine costumes are not generally worn for everyday activities. They are kept for special occasions and especially to delight the tourists. However, older people are more likely to wear a costume, and there are still remote villages, for example in the Hèrens Valley, where traditional dress is regularly worn.

The Alpine region is characterized by its music and folk dancing. Traditional songs are linked closely to the herding of cattle and goats. Simple songs are thought to have developed from a male herder singing the names of his animals, as he rounded them up. This singing, including unusually high notes, is called yodelling. It is rarely heard in the mountains today but is more likely to occur at cultural folk music gatherings. This is also true of the gigantic alphorn – a 4-metre long wooden horn that was once used to call cattle from the pastures. Other traditional Alpine instruments, such as the accordian and the zither, are played much more frequently, although often they are for the benefit of tourists in restaurants and bars. Folk dances are still popular with local people, although fewer young people go to them. They are more likely to be interested in discos and pop concerts.

A flower-filled meadow, high in the Alps. These are becoming less and less common: oilseed rape is becoming increasingly common instead.

Alpine traditions are declining as the way of life changes in the Alps. Farming practices are changing rapidly. The custom of most fam- ilies keeping a few grazing animals is dying out, as people have found other forms of employment. The development of large super- markets means that it is no longer necessary for people to keep animals for self-sufficiency.

Hay meadows are also much less common than they used to be. Instead of a bright, flower-filled meadow, there may be a single crop of clover or oilseed rape. To keep these crops free of weeds and insect pests, Alpine farmers often take advantage of the strong chemicals available as herbicides or pesti- cides. These products have harmful effects on the food chain.

In these ways, Alpine farming is catching up with modern practices used elsewhere, and the environment is experiencing the dis-

advantages as well as the benefits of new types of farming technology.

Transport is another example of the con- trasts that exist in the Alps today. Car owner- ship is widespread, and traffic congestion occurs in many places, especially on popular tourist routes in France and Bavaria. Peaceful villages are disturbed as busy roads carry a stream of lorries, transporting goods across the Alps. In spite of this, there are still some Alpine villages that are inaccessible by road. The only way to reach them is by funicular railway from the valley floor.

So the Alps are a curious mixture of old and new, the present and the past. Although some parts seem far removed from modern life, the region is not immune to today's prob- lems. Near the edge of the Alps in Switzer- land lies Zurich, a large, modern city. Here common twentieth-century problems such as drug use and AIDS are all-too familiar.

Hay Meadows

Traditional hay meadows are much less common than they used to be. Such meadows contain a rich mixture of grasses and wild flowers, including ox-eye daisies, buttercups, clovers, bellflowers, scabious, knapweeds, wild orchids and even lilies. The many kinds of flowers attract pollinating insects such as bees, butterflies and hoverflies, as well as plant-eating beetles and grasshoppers. These insects, in turn, attract small predators, such as ground beetles, ladybirds and spiders. Mice and birds feed in the meadows, and these small animals are preyed on by kestrels, buzzards and owls. So a hay meadow supports hundreds of species of plants and animals.

Fields with single crops such as clover or oilseed rape are less time-consuming to manage than hay meadows, and some farmers think they produce a better yield of animal feed. However, single-crop fields are not as good for wildlife. To keep out unwanted weeds from the main crop, farmers often spray them with herbicides. And because the single-crop field can quickly be invaded by pests such as aphids, farmers spray the crop with strong chemical pesticides. The poisons in these sprays not only kill the insect pests, but they also pass up the food chain, killing beetles, mice and birds.

As the traditional landscape of the Alpine slopes changes, nature conservation groups are calling for the return of the these meadow. Not only are these meadows an important habitat for many species of plants and animals; many people also think they are more in keeping with the Alpine landscape than large fields of single crops.

· FACING · THE · FUTURE

In this book we have looked at the wide variety of places and people that make up the Alps. We have seen that it is a region of many contrasts, a unique combination of traditional and modern life. Certainly the region has changed a good deal since the 1950s, but what of the future? As with most parts of the world, a number of challenges will need to be met in the future.

This small rural community in Italy could be threatened by economic changes in the Alps.

▲
Many young people have left Alpine villages for cities such as Zurich, where there are jobs and more things to do in their spare time.

THE FUTURE FOR PEOPLE

One challenge is to build a secure economic future for the people of the Alps. Although tourism has brought wealth to the region, it has not created enough jobs for everyone. Today many young people are leaving the Alpine villages where they were born to work in larger towns, which provide jobs in large shops, banks, insurance and so on. Local officials in Alpine communities are concerned about this trend, because it leaves unbalanced communities, with a high proportion of older people. A healthy community needs a balance of old and young, including families with children. Without this mix, communities will decline in the future.

Solving this problem is not easy. It would help if existing large employers, such as insurance companies, could be persuaded to relocate from big cities such as Zurich into one of the towns in the Alps. It would also help if there were greater investment in the local communities. Some local people feel that too much investment has gone into facilities for tourists, and not enough into amenities for the resident population – better roads, health centres, restaurants, cinemas, social centres, schools and so on.

The survival of Alpine customs and traditions is another unknown factor for the future. If traditional communities break up because young people do not stay there, there is little chance that traditions will survive. Tourism has been an excuse in some places to keep up traditions such as accordion music and folk dancing. But the true test of traditions is whether they have a meaning to the local people, and whether these people can invest the time and energy to keep them alive for future generations.

THE FUTURE FOR THE ENVIRONMENT

Another challenge is how best to protect the environment. The unique scenery and wildlife of the Alps is under threat in places because of the pressure to develop the region. Skiing can cause a good deal of damage. In the large French ski resort of Val d'Isère, thousands of skiers have carved a network of scars into the mountainside. Once the snow melts in spring, the damage becomes clear. The scars not only look unsightly; they can also cause soil erosion. The good soil becomes dusty and blows away, leaving dry, bare slopes where no vegetation will grow. Skiers are also known to have triggered avalanches as they cut through deep snow.

Loss of forests is another problem for the Alps. Whether cleared for settlements, agriculture or ski runs, the lower slopes have lost much of their natural forest cover. Trees play an important part in the water cycle, and their roots help to anchor soil, preventing soil erosion. Clearing forests can create erosion problems, and it also destroys the habitat of woodland plants and animals.

Forests in the Alps are also dying because of the effects of acid rain. The rainfall turns acid because of the build-up of sulphur dioxide and nitrogen oxides, caused by pollution from industry and vehicles. Air pollution from industrial centres in Europe is thought to be responsible for damage to forests in the Alps. Most of the trees are conifers, which react to the acid rainwater by shedding their needles and producing too many cones, before dying. Acid rain cannot be solved by the people of the Alps alone; it is a problem common to the many European countries that produce air pollution, and will be solved only by strict controls on discharges from industry and cars.

A patch of conifer forest has been cleared, perhaps to create a new ski run or a field for crops, leaving the remains of old trees.

Dying Forests

In the early 1980s, people began to notice changes in the forests that cover the lower slopes of the Alps. Many conifers, such as spruce, fir and pine, had yellow or spotted needles, and some trees had bare branches where leaves had dropped. On closer investigation, the problem was found to be more severe in the eastern Alps than in the west. While moderate tree damage was reported around Grenoble in France and the Alto Adige (South Tyrol) of Italy, in Switzerland and Germany over 60 per cent of the trees in Alpine forests were affected. What was causing this devastation?

Many people were quick to point the finger at acid rain, which has been blamed for forest damage in Scandinavia, western Europe and North America. Certainly levels of air pollution are much higher today than in the 1960s. And as westerly winds blow from the Atlantic eastwards over Europe's industrial cities, they pick up increasing amounts of air pollution. More pollution is found in the eastern Alps, which could explain the higher rate of forest damage there.

However, the case against acid rain is not watertight. Other factors can also cause the death of trees. For example, in 1987 many Swiss conifers in mountain forests developed reddish needles. The media blamed the damage on acid rain. However, researchers found that the main cause was a cycle of freezing weather and thaws, caused by alternating cold Arctic winds and the warm Föhn wind.

Whatever the cause, the death of Alpine forests has aroused strong feelings in the local people. In Germany a campaign was launched to stop the forests dying. Now the various Alpine countries have research programmes into air pollution and acid-rain damage. Scientists measure pollution levels in the trees and monitor complex ecological and meteorological conditions. Although they cannot be sure of the exact cause of forest damage, it seems likely that a combination of factors are to blame: air pollution, climate changes (from drought to frost), altitude, insect pests and attacks by fungi.

These German trees have been damaged by acid rain.

A reservoir created by damming a river has flooded a whole valley.

Another problem concerns the construction of hydroelectric schemes in the Alps. Although these produce clean electricity, they are not without harmful effects on the environment. When a reservoir is created, by damming a river, a large area of the valley is flooded. Sometimes people have had to leave their homes behind because their village would be submerged when the reservoir filled with water. Plant communities are also lost when the valley is flooded, and the wildlife that depended on the river are affected. Some people feel that the reservoirs created in this way look unattractive and artificial, especially with the towering wall of concrete that forms the dam.

All the above problems result from the pressure on the Alpine environment by people. There is a dilemma here because local people need the money brought by tourist development, and yet this can spoil the environment. Likewise, local people and tourists use up electricity, and so energy schemes are necessary in the Alps even though not everyone likes them.

If the Alpine area continues to be developed without sufficient thought for the environment, the whole area will suffer in the future. The solution must lie in reaching a compromise between the needs of the people and the environment.

Back in 1972, in Germany, the Bavarian local government started to try to solve this problem. It classified land into areas that could be developed for tourism in the future, existing tourist areas that could be sensitively developed, and areas where no development would be allowed at all.

An ibex climbs a rocky outcrop in the Italian Gran Paradiso national park. The creation of national parks is one way in which the Alpine environment could be preserved.

LEAVING ROOM FOR WILDLIFE

Already some areas of the Alps have been set aside as national parks. These are protected areas where wildlife can live in peace, free from the threat of hunting and habitat loss. There are national parks in all the major Alpine countries. The French Vanoise park adjoins the Gran Paradiso park in Italy, forming a large area of protected land in the western Alps. Similarly, in the central Alps the Italian Stelvio park adjoins the Swiss National Park. National parks in Germany, Austria and the former Yugoslavia, together with a number of smaller nature reserves, mean that throughout the Alps there are some areas where wildlife comes first. Some of them protect unique species, such as the ancient forests of stone pines growing near the Aletsch Glacier in Switzerland.

National parks not only protect species from possible danger; they also aim to increase the numbers of plants and animals. The Gran Paradiso park in Italy has been successful in increasing the numbers of ibex, which at one point were threatened with extinction. National parks are good for people as well as wildlife because they give people the chance to see the wealth of plants and animals that can flourish in the Alps.

The national parks have shown that all the different countries that share the Alps have a common concern for the future of the region's wildlife. All these countries must also face the challenge of providing a bright future for their people. It is likely that the various countries will have different priorities for the future. Whatever the uncertainties facing the Alps, one thing is sure: the majestic mountains will continue to arouse wonder and awe.

GLOSSARY

Altitude Height above sea-level.

Archaeological To do with the study of human history and prehistory.

Avalanche A 'landslide' of snow down a mountainside.

Cable car A passenger cabin suspended from overhead cables that is pulled up and down a mountainside.

Candlemas A Christian festival that is celebrated in February every year.

Canton A district of Switzerland.

Communal Owned and shared by a group.

Conifers Trees that bear cones and have needle-like leaves. Most have these leaves all year.

Cumulonimbus A tall, flat-topped cloud formation, associated with thunderstorms.

Deciduous Trees that shed their leaves in the autumn.

Dialect A local form of a language with its own vocabulary, grammar and pronounciation. Often dialects are spoken but not written.

Environment All the conditions that surround us, including air, water, soil, plants and animals.

Eurasia Europe and Asia.

Extinction The dying-out of a species.

Funicular railway Passenger carriages that travel up and down a mountainside on sloping rails. They are pulled along by a moving cable.

Geology The study of the earth's rocks.

Glaciated Once covered by a glacier.

Habitat The natural home of particular species of plants and animals.

Hanging valley A high-level side valley that joins a main valley above the level of its floor.

Igneous rocks Rocks formed from molten lava (magma) from the earth's crust.

Industrial Revolution The expansion of European industry in the late eighteenth and early nineteenth centuries.

Labour-intensive Involving many workers.

Metamorphosed Describes a rock that has been changed under heat or pressure. For example, marble is metamorphosed limestone.

Moraine Rocks and debris deposited by a glacier.

Neanderthals A prehistoric people who lived in Europe 130,000–30,000 years ago.

Pollinating Fertilizing with pollen, a powder produced by flowers.

Scree A layer of eroded rock fragments found high up on mountains.

Sedimentary rocks Rocks formed from layers of compressed sediment, such as sand or fossilized sea creatures.

Soil erosion The wearing away of exposed soil by wind and water. This happens once the protective cover of plants has been removed.

Spa town A health resort with a spring of mineral water.

Subtropical Parts of the world just outside the tropics with a warm, mild climate.

BOOKS TO READ

Acid Rain (Conserving our World) by John Baines (Wayland 1989)

Europe and the Environment by David Stent (Wayland 1991)

Farming and the Environment (Conserving our World) by Mark Lambert (Wayland 1991)

Farming in Europe by David Flint (Wayland 1991)

Mountains (Ecology Watch) by Alan Collinson (Cloverleaf/Evans Brothers 1991)

Mountains (Our World) by Keith Lye (Wayland 1987)

Tourism in Europe by David Flint (Wayland 1992)

The Usborne Book of the Earth by Fiona Watt (Usborne 1992)

Vanishing Habitats (Survival) by Noel Simon (Aladdin/Franklin Watts 1987)

USEFUL ADDRESSES

Council for Environmental Education
School of Education
University of Reading
London Road
Reading RG1 5AQ

Friends of the Earth (Australia)
PO Box A474
Sydney
NSW 2001

Friends of the Earth (Canada)
251 Laurier Avenue
W Suite 701
Ottowa
Ontario K1P 5J6

Friends of the Earth (New Zealand)
PO Box 5599
Wellesley Street
Auckland West

Friends of the Earth (UK)
26–28 Underwood Street
London N1 7JQ

International Centre for Conservation Education
Greenfield House
Guiting Power
Cheltenham
Gloucester GL54 5TZ

WWF UK (World Wide Fund for Nature)
Panda House
Weyside Park
Godalming
Surrey GU7 1XR

INDEX